Miracles in Celtic History

3 Books in 1

"Irish Slaves in America"

"Bangor –
Light of the World"

"Child Prophets of the
Huguenots"

Published by
Good News Fellowship Ministries
220 Sleepy Creek Rd
Macon, GA 31210

format by Lisa Walters Buck
info@lisawbuckdesign.com
www.lisawbuckdesign.com

Table of Contents

IRISH SLAVES IN AMERICA

BANGOR LIGHT OF THE WORLD

BANGOR LIGHT OF THE WORLD

Irish Slaves

in America

Kathie Walters

Irish Slaves in America
Copyright © 2014 by Kathie Walters

Printed in the United States of America

Published by
Good News Fellowship Ministries
220 Sleepy Creek Rd
Macon, GA 31210

format by Lisa Walters Buck
info@lisawbuckdesign.com
www.lisawbuckdesign.com

Many thanks to Beverly Pickering, San Antonio, TX for helping me gather these facts.

Table of Contents

Introduction

These are merely notes to help you understand what happened to the Irish slaves. Most people in America are ignorant of the huge indignity and cruel treatment of the Irish Catholics. Why is it so hidden? Why isn't it taught in school as many Americans are from these very immigrant people who were forced to come here and many died in the process? I wonder if the British Government has ever apologized for the awful work James I, or Oliver Cromwell and such who saw the Irish as dogs. I hope this will help you understand and break the curses that came on the land.

The Background of Irish Slaves in America

At the beginning of the 17th Century, in the reign of James I of England, England faced a problem: what to do with the Irish Catholics. They had been practicing genocide against the Irish since the reign of Elizabeth, but they couldn't kill them all. Some had been banished, and some had gone into voluntary exile, but there were still just too many of them. So James I encouraged the sale of the Irish as slaves to the New World colonies not only to America but Barbados the West Indies, and South America in 1612. The English deliberately targeted the Irish, and the Scots, because at that time there was no distinction made between the Irish and the Scots.

The English had an old and virulent contempt for the Irish. In 1574, when an expedition led by the Earl of Essex slaughtered the entire population of Rathlin Island in Ulster, totaling 600 people, one of the members of the expedition, Edward Barkley wrote, "How godly a deed it is to overthrow so wicked a race the world may judge: for my part I think there cannot be a greater sacrifice to God." (Quoted by Nicholas Canny in <u>The Ideology of English Colonization from Ireland to America</u>, William and Mary Quarterly, 1973.)

When the English targeted the Irish, women and children were especially vulnerable. Slavers snatched up children and carted them off to prisons or workhouses on spurious charges, such as 'vagrancy.' When the parents finally discovered where they were -- if they did -- and tried to claim them to take them home, the jailers demanded that they pay for the food the children had eaten while imprisoned. If they couldn't, as was usually the case, the children were then transported and sold as slaves.

In 1641, when the Irish tried to shake off the English rule, chaos resulted. As a result, in the 11 years following the revolt was known as the Confederation War, the Irish population fell from 1,466,000 to 616,000. Over 550,000 Irishmen were killed, and at least 300,000 were sold as slaves. After the 1649 conquest, Sir William Petty estimated that one-sixth of all Irish men had been shipped away and sold abroad. That made a lot of Irish women and children also very easily available to the slave trade.

Of course, the men were not allowed to take their wives and children. The women and children who were left homeless and destitute were themselves rounded up and sold as salves. Sometimes they were sent to prisons or workhouses, and deported from there. Sometimes they were just snatched up, either

4

from the side of the road or from their beds, and spirited away. It is from this time the word "kidnapped" became such a common word. And yet even though it did not seem that things could get worse than under James I, things got much worse indeed under the control of OLIVER CROMWELL.

In 1652, Cromwell instigated the Ethnic Cleansing of Ireland. He demanded that all Irish people were to resettle west of Shannon, in arid, uninhabitable land, or be transported to the West Indies, thus losing the lands that they had possessed for many generations. The majority of the Irish refused to relocate peaceably, knowing that they couldn't survive if they did There was no grazing land for sheep, no viable land to plant crops. Cromwell did whatever was necessary to see the Irish were removed, because their land had been promised to the troops as payment for putting down the Irish rebellion. These Irish became outlaws on their own land.

By Cromwell's death, at least 100,000 Irish men, women, and children had been sold in the West Indies, Virginia, and New England. The men were generally sold for life if they were political prisoners; the women and children were supposed to be sold for a certain period of years, after which, they were to be free, should they survive that long. But they were often "bred" and their children were slaves permanently. Very few mothers would leave their children so in that sense, they too were slaves too as long as they lived.

Aboard Ship

Whether black, white, indentured, or enslaved, the cargo was carried the same way. Once aboard ship, the chances of actually making it to the new destination were not great. The conditions of the slaves onboard ship were miserable. No one really cared if they lived or died, as they were cheap and plentiful. One eye-witness described typical conditions thus: 'There is onboard these ships terrible misery, stench, fumes horror, vomiting, many kinds of sea-sickness, fever, dysentery, headache, heat, constipation boils, scurvy, cancer, mouth rot and the like, all of which comes from old and sharply salted food and meat, also from very bad and foul water, so that many die miserable.....Children from 1 to 7 years rarely survive the voyage.'

Marcus Jernigan writing in <u>Slavery and the Beginnings of Industrialism in the American Colonies</u>, stated: "The voyage over often repeated the horrors of the famous 'middle passage' of slavery fame. An average cargo was 300, but the shipmaster, for greater profit, would sometimes crowd as many as 600 into a small vessel...The mortality under such circumstances was tremendous, sometimes more than half." Mittenberger (an eyewitness) says he saw 32 children thrown into the ocean during one voyage. These conditions did not improve as long as the slavery trade lasted.

In the article "The Forgotten Slaves: Whites in Servitude in Early America and Industrial Britain," by Michael A. Hoffman II, he states that as late as 1855, Fredrick Law Olmsted, the premiere landscape artist of his day was traveling in Alabama and saw black men throwing huge bale of hay carelessly down into the hold of a cargo ship. The hold was filled with white men. Hoffman claims that Olmsted asked about this and was told by a ship worker, 'Oh the niggers are worth too much to be risked here; but if the Paddies are knocked overboard or get their back broke, nobody loses anything.'

Hoffman also quotes a study of white slave transport in the Parliamentary Petition of 1659, in which it was reported that the Irish slaves were kept in the hold aboard ship for 2 weeks before the ship even set sail, and were then chained at the neck and the legs and 'all the way locked up under decks...amongst horses.'

Once every two weeks at sea the (indentured servant) passengers received a small allowance of bread. One man and his wife, having eaten their bread in eight days, staggered before the captain and begged him to throw them overboard, for they would otherwise starve before the next bread day. The captain laughed in their faces, while the ship's mate, even more of a brute, gave them a bag of sand and told them to eat that. The couple did die before the next ration of bread, but the captain charged the other passengers for the bread the two would have eaten if they had survived.'

Hoffman continues, describing the environment in those times: Even in the later days of the trade in white labor, when indentured servitude was the rule rather than actual slavery, and after indentured servitude gave way to contract labor, things did not improve aboard ship.

In the 1840's, during the Potato Famine, when hordes of poor Irish came to America either as indentured servants or to work for, literally, slave wages, they faced terrible times at sea and many did not make it. Conditions were usually worse aboard ship for the Irish at that time than for the African slaves, as the slaves were a more valuable commodity.

In the most disastrous year of all, 1847, about 20 percent of the huge number of immigrants caused by the famine died en route to America or upon landing. This was about 40,000 dead."

Barbados

The Irish had a tendency to die in the heat, and were not as well suited to the work as African slaves, but African slaves had to be bought. Irish slaves could be kidnapped if there weren't enough prisoners or former inhabitants of workhouses, and of course, it was easy enough to make Irish prisoners by manufacturing some petty crime or other. This made the Irish the preferred 'livestock' for English slave traders for 200 years.

In the 1650's England captured Jamaica from the Spanish, and suddenly had a huge island to populate and make profitable. There were not enough workers so then Cromwell fell back o his usual strategy and sent his 'man-catchers' to round up some more Irish to transport. In 1656, Cromwell's Council of State ordered 1000 Irish girls and 1000 Irish boys to be rounded up and transported to Jamaica and sold as slaves to the English planters there. This is one of the few official records of slave activity, as most was unrecorded. Henry Cromwell wrote to an official in Jamaica, 'Though we must use force in taking them up....it is not in the least doubtful that you may have as many of them as you see fit.

With slavery an accepted practice of not only nobility but the royal family itself, there was no hope for relief for the Irish who either would die of starvation at home, in a workhouse or prison, or on a ship chained in a hold or in a strange land. They would also be beaten, worked beyond exhaustion, exposed to tropical diseases, and, in the case of the women, probably raped. To live free was a rare thing for any Irish person of that time.

In 1695, the Penal Laws were passed which punished Irish Catholics for their support of the Stuarts against James II of England. In the Great Hunger; Ireland 1845-1849, Cecil Woodhall-Smith explains the meaning and results of these laws. A contemporary tellingly wrote that the laws had the express purpose of reducing the Irish Catholics to 'insignificant slaves, fit for nothing but to hew sod and draw water.

Irish Catholics could not vote, hold office, or purchase land. Upon the death of the head of the family, their estate was to be divided among all the sons of the family, unless the eldest became Protestant, when he would inherit everything. Catholics could not attend school or send their children away from Ireland to attend school. Practicing Catholicism was a crime, and to be a priest was illegal and highly dangerous. Thus at this time in history, it was the Irish Catholics who were most likely to become slaves.

The story of the Irish is a summary of all the ways in which the Penal Laws forced the Irish into a life of crime, leading thousands to be arrested and shipped away as criminals or vagrants to become slaves in the West Indies, Barbados and the Colonies:

- He was forbidden to receive education.

- He was forbidden to enter a profession.

- He was forbidden to hold public office.

- He was forbidden to engage in trade or commerce.

- He was forbidden to live in a corporate town or within five miles.

- He was forbidden to own a horse of greater value that £5.00.

- He was forbidden to purchase land.

- He was forbidden to accept a mortgage on land in security for a loan.

- He was forbidden to vote.

- He was forbidden to keep any arms for his protection.

- He was forbidden to hold a life annuity.

- He was forbidden to buy land from a Protestant.

- He was forbidden to receive a gift of land from a Protestant.

- He was forbidden to inherit anything from a Protestant.

- He was forbidden to rent any land that was worth more than 30 shillings a year.

- He was forbidden to reap from his land any profit exceeding a third of the rent.

- He could not be guardian to a child.

- He could not, when dying, leave his infant children under Catholic guardianship.

- He could not attend Catholic worship.

- He was compelled by law to attend Protestant worship.

- He could not himself educate his child.

- He could not send his child to a Catholic teacher.

- He could not employ a Catholic teacher to come to his child.

- He could not send his child abroad to receive education.

These Penal Laws stayed in effect, for the most part, until 1820's!

In 1701, the Calendar of State Papers, Colonial Series of 1701, reported that there were 25,000 slaves in the West Indies, 21,700 of them white The majority of these would have been Irish, although there were also Scots and Dutchmen among them.

In a book written in 1932 by Joseph J. Williams, Whence the "Black Irish" of Jamaica, he reports that the slaves worked from 6 AM until 6 PM.

In the West Indies, the African and Irish slaves were housed together, but because the African slaves were much more costly, it is argued that they were treated better than the Irish slaves. An Irish slave was much more likely to endure such treatment as having his hands and feet set on fire for even a small infraction.

The land owners also began to breed the Irish women with the African male slaves to make lighter skinned slaves, because the lighter skinned slaves were more desirable and could be sold for more money.

This practice became so common that, in 1681, the English government passed an act forbidding the practice of mating Irish slave women to African slave men for the purpose of producing slaves for sale. This legislation had nothing to do with morality or racial consideration, but was strictly for monetary interests. The practice was causing the Royal African Company to lose profits, because they could not sell as many slaves if the planters were providing attractive merchandise themselves, or growing their own slaves! (Despite these concerns, from 1680 to 1688, the Royal African Company still managed to sell 249 shiploads of slaves to the Indies and American Colonies, over 60,000 Irish and Africans. The profit was tremendous, despite the over 14,000 lost at sea).

One advantage the Irish slaves had over the African slaves was due to their literacy, they were rarely put in the fields. The Irish died of heat, misuse and disease. Those who tried to run away were often branded with an "FT" For Fugitive Traitor on their foreheads. (The Republican News, 1997) Instead, they were often used as house servants, accountants, and teachers. But the gentility of the service did not correlate to the punishment for infractions. It was in 1667 that Parliament passed, "The Act to Regulate Slaves on British Plantations", which designated certain acceptable punishments, but it applied only to Christian slaves. The Irish, who were Catholic, were not considered Christian by the Protestant planters. Indeed, any follower of the Pope was considered the enemy of Christianity and there were no laws to protect them, even from being beaten to death should the owner so choose.

Religious persecution was the source for much abuse against the Irish. The Irish Catholics were not allowed to observe Mass or any other Catholic ritual. The denial of the right to practice their religion was a very difficult thing for the Irish slaves to bear. They constantly sought to be allowed religious freedom. A 1997 article in The Republican News, an Irish paper, recounts how 150 Irish Catholics were caught practicing their religion and were subsequently rounded up and taken to a small, uninhabited island called Crab and left there to starve to death.

While many of the Irish were sold into service for only about 10 years, assuming they survived that long, in the West Indies their children were born slaves for life. The planters knew that many of the mothers would remain in servitude to remain with their children even after their service was technically up, so they would be able to keep both the children and the mothers.

The West Indies

Despite is being in the middle of the harsh times there was some Irish survivors. Cromwell sent many of those survivors to Barbados. After wiping out the entire garrison at Drogheda in 1649, Cromwell stated, "I do not think 30 of their whole number escaped with their lives. Those that did are in safe custody in the Barbados."

In that same year, Irish slaves in Barbados revolted. The revolt failed, and they were hanged, drawn, and quartered. Then their heads were cut off and impaled on pikes and displayed as a warning to other slaves who might be tempted to try to gain freedom.

At this time, Cromwell's son, Henry, also rounded up 1,000 "Irish wenches" to be sold in Barbados, and 2,000 Irish boys between the ages of 12 and 14. "Who knows," he wrote, "but it might be a means to make them Englishmen."

Due to yellow fever, malaria, overwork and maltreatment, between 33% and 50% of the indentured servants in Barbados died before they reached the end of their sentence of servitude.

Barbados was so full of hate and oppression, the abuse on the island was notibally more harsh than other areas. It was common practice for the slave traders to kidnap people from their beds at night and taken to Barbados. W.E.B. Dubois noted that "Even young Irish peasants were hunted down as men hunt down game, and were forcibly put aboard ship, and sold to plantations in Barbados."

In an attempt to further parade his control over the Irish, Cromwell also had decreed that Irish Catholics were forbidden to attend Catholic services. Many priests were transported and sold as slaves. Any

Catholic in Ireland who refused to attend a Protestant service could be fined, and if the person could not raise the money, he would be transported and sold as a slave in Barbados.

Making them English or Christian (Protestant) was often the excuse for selling these Irish Catholics into slavery, entirely overlooking the fact that they would probably die or suffer fates worse than death before that happened.

George Washington visited Barbados in 1751 and stayed for six weeks. The future President of the US, who was himself a slave owner, said at the time, 'In the cool of the evening we rode in the country and were perfectly enraptured with the beautiful scenery which every side presented our view. The fields of cane, corn, fruit trees in a delightful green...' Without doubt, he never gave a thought to the white and black slaves who kept those fields so green with their sweat and blood.

To this day, many of the inhabitants of Barbados have Irish surnames; Gill and Murphy being the most common.

The Americas

The Irish were not only sold in the West Indies and Barbados they were also sold in the Colonies, as well. It is important to remember that in the 1600's and most of the 1700's, America was merely an extension of England, loyal British subjects of the King and bound by English law and custom. When there was a need for labor, the Colonies embraced the same notions of indentured servitude and convict labor as the British settlements elsewhere had found so useful.

As early as 1618, a law was passed to allow street children, both Irish and English, to be sent to Virginia.

100 children were sent in 1619. 100 more in 1620, and in 1622, after the Indian Massacre of 350 Colonists, 100 more were sent with the reinforcements. From that point on, the exportation of children was accomplished either by legal means through various Poor Laws, by charitable organizations, or by being kidnapped or spirited away, with those being sent illegally by far the majority.

In the 1650's over 100,000 Irish Catholic children between the ages of 10 and 14 were taken from their parents and sold as slaves, many to Virginia and New England. Unbelievably, from 1651 to 1660 there were more Irish slaves in America than the entire non-slave population of the colonies!

In 1692, a reporter from an English newspaper, The Flying Post, claimed that he saw 200 kidnapped boys being held in the cargo hold of a ship for transportation to the colonies.

However, it was not only children who were sent as slaves to the Colonies in the 1600's. Men and women were sent as well, either as political prisoners or from the workhouses and prisons, or captured and spirited away in the same way that the children were, sometimes right out of their beds.

In Irish Immigrants in the Land of Canaan, written and edited by Kerby Miller, Arnold Schrier, Bruce Boling, and David Doyle, the number of immigrants is substantially higher. They report that 14,000 were shipped directly from Ireland in the 1700's, and that many of the 50,000 shipped from England during that time were also Irish. Most of England during that time were also Irish. Most of them served year sentences in the states, mostly on plantations in Maryland and Virginia.

Most were males in their teens and early 20's, and most were unskilled and illiterate laborers or craftsmen. This was a time when almost every European immigrant landed in America in bondage and at least 9 out of 10 Irish. While only about 10% of these indentured servants ran away, for the Irish the percentage was much higher.

Thomas Addis Emmet, in Ireland Under English Rule, published in 1902, stated that 'between 20,000 and 30,000 men and women who were taken prisoner were sold in the American colonies as slaves, with no respect to their former station in life.

Richard Hofsadter claims that almost 30,000 felons were transported to the colonies as servants in the eighteenth century, about two-thirds of whom went to Virginia and Maryland

Other starving and homeless people were lied to or tricked into signing documents agreeing to be sold in America for a term of years to work as slave labor, and these became indentured servants, Agents, called spirits, would search for the hungry, dusty souls struggling to survive, and offer them dinner and drink. The agent would then cajole the individual into signing a paper which he or she could not read, hustle the victim to a safe place where, with others, they would be held without a chance of escape until a ship was available. Of course, any drunk on the street was even easier prey. Children were easiest of all They could either be bribed with sweets or simply overpowered and carried away, and sold until they reached the age of 21.

Men and women alike, for the entire 17th Century, from 1600 until 1699, there were many more Irish sold as slaves to the Colonies than Africans.

In Irish of the Inside: In search of the Soul of Irish America, Tom Hayden quotes Thomas Addis Emmett as saying that these Irish '...were sent abroad into slavery in the West Indies, Virginia and New England, that they might thus lose their faith and all knowledge of their nationality for in most instances even their names were changed.' These political prisoners former homeless, and denizens of workhouses and prisons were often not offered contracts stating that they could work work their way to freedom. They were also often branded with the initials of the ship that brought them to be sold. This was a way of breaking the spirit, literally taking away the identity of the person. Denying them the right to practice their religion or any of their cultural rituals was another way of trying to get these new slaves to accept their fate.

"There was a great demand for women in the early years of the colonies, and the purpose they were to serve was no secret. In 'the Women's History of the World, Rosalind Miles describes how these women were treated. They were sold, in Jamestown, for '120 pounds of best tobacco' and thus bound to the seller for wife, servant, or mistress for life. Within two years, the price for a woman had rocketed to 150 pounds."

The Specific Case of Indentured Servants

The state of Georgia is a unique case in the colonies, as it was founded entirely as a debtors' colony, and all of the earliest settlers were people who were sent there from England because they owed debts they could not pay and were sent to Georgia rather than being sent to the overcrowded Debtors' Prisons in England.

This pamphlet is quoted in David Olin Relin's article, — Misery, written for Scholastic Search. He goes on to explain that the miserable treatment which most indentured servants actually received, having signed away all of their rights for a number of years, was a secret that the company closely guarded. Letters home were rigidly censored, and a law was passed against anyone who should — dare to detract slander or utter unseemly speeches against the company, with the penalty being public execution!

In the colonies, laws were sometimes passed to try to make conditions aboard the ships bringing the servants in less horrible. The laws that Pennsylvania passed in 1750, according to Wikipedia, indicate how onerous conditions must otherwise have been: 'According to the statutes of the act, six feet of — Bed Place was required for every four.' In 1765 the legislature passed a supplemental law that added a — 'vertical standard to — horizontal space specified in the previous act, stipulating three feet nine inches of — Bed Place at the forepart of the ship and two feet nine inches in the cabin and steerage.

Six feet of space for four grown people with less than 4 feet of room to sit or stand in, was considered a great improvement. The explanation, of course, is that the laws were not intended to create comfort, but merely to decrease the spread of contagious disease, which not only interfered with the increase in the work force but caused colonists to fear that the disease might spread from the servants to the colonist themselves.

Below Is Also Quoted Aboard Ship

Indentured servants did not fare any better on the trip from England to America, which took at least 7 weeks, than slaves did. Here is a description by Gottlieb Mittelberger, writing in 1754 in On the Misfortune of Indentured Servant: 'But during the voyage there is on bard these ships terrible misery, stench, fumes. horror, vomiting, many kinds of sea-sickness, fever, dysentery, heat, constipation, boils, scurvy, cancer, mouth-rot, and the like, all of which come from old and sharply salted food and meat, also from very bad and foul water so that many die miserably.

The Next is New

Gottlieb explains how auctions were carried out on ships that landed in Philadelphia. He describes how merchants, businessmen and plantation owners would come even from long distances to come aboard ship and choose from the cargo those servants they thought would best suit their purposes, and negotiate for their services for a term of years. Often husband, wives, and children were sold to different owners and might not see each other again for many years, if ever.

A weaver from London witnessed an auction of Irish slaves in Williamsburg in 1758 and gave this description;

"They all was set in row, near 100 men and women and the planter come down the country to buy...I never see such parcels of poor wretches in my life some almost naked and what had clothes was as black as chimney sweeps, and almost starved by the ill-usage of their passage by the captain, for they are used no better than many negro slaves and sold in the same manner as horses or cows in our market or fair."

Black historian Lerone Bennett, Jr., in The Shaping of Black America, describes how Irishmen were sold in North Carolina in the 1640's for 35 barrels of turpentine. In 1755, the governor of Maryland wrote that:'The planters' fortunes here consist in the number of their servants (who are purchased at high rates) much as the estates of an English farmers do in the multitude of cattle.

Even when they survived the journey, many of these people, who were only "indentured servants" and surely not "slaves" did not get to appreciate their survival long. In 1671, the governor of Virginia estimated that four fifths of the indentured servants died shortly after they arrived, from heat, disease, ill-use, and overwork. They were poorly fed and clothed in many cases and, even when freed, were poverty-stricken and unskilled, with little chance to become more than common laborers, or in the case of the women, cooks, kitchen maids, or prostitutes. The person, once bought, was not simply consigned to work for his owner for the period of time contracted, but to be that person's slave and do their bidding in all things or be punished just like any other slave, as this Maryland law from the late 1600's indicates.

Irish servants could also be willed to others, just like any other property.

Maryland, Virginia, Pennsylvania, Delaware, and New Jersey received more indentured servants than any other colonies in the 17th century. About 80% of all European immigrants at that time were indentured, and while some were "redemptionists" who freely agreed to work a certain number of years to escape from extreme poverty in their home country, and others were not Irish, the majority were either political prisoners, the destitute or homeless (including traveling musicians and peddlers, who owned no land), or those who had been kidnapped and transported, and more of them were Irish than any other ethnicity.

Of all the colonies, Virginia seems to have the most recorded laws concerning indentured servants. For instance, in 1705, the Virginia General Assembly made this declaration: 'All servants imported and brought into the country....who were not Christians in their native country....shall be accounted and be slaves...if any slave resists his master....correcting such slave, and shall happen to be killed in such correction...the master shall be free of all punishment.... as if such accident never happened.

Remember that the Irish, who were predominantly Catholic, were not considered "Christian" at this time. And — resisting the master could be so much as a spoken protest, a look, or simply not moving fast enough for the master's liking. So if the servant (not slave!) were then beaten to death or punished in some other way that led to death, the master was not guilty of murder, or even a misdemeanor, but the — accident might as well never have happened! Of course, the other colonies also received indentured servants, not all of whom were Catholic. In Boston in 1730, an announcement appearing in the Boston, News Letter for an auction of Irish boys., and a group of women connects from Belfast was sold in Boston in 1749. As late as 1860, two thirds of the servants in Boston were Irish.

The average age of the indentured servants who came willingly due to homelessness or poverty or who were kidnapped and — spirited' to America of the West Indies was 15-20, while the — convicts (many of whom had committed crimes such as stealing a chicken or poaching a rabbit for food) were usually between 20 and 30 years of age. Younger children, however, sometimes appear in the records, some as young as 6 or 7 years of age, and women were always desirable as long as they were past puberty.

Indentured servants were forbidden to marry during their servitude. However, it could still become a matter of legal debate. Virginia, in fact, enacted a law in 1662, that if an indentured woman had a child by her master, she had to serve an additional two years as a slave to the church wardens: 'that each woman servant gotten with child by her master shall after her time by indenture or custom is expired be by the church wardens of the parish where she lived when she was brought to bed of such bastard, sold for two years.

There were occupations which used almost exclusively white, usually Irish, or Asian labor in because of the danger and hardship of the work, as black slaves were too expensive to be as disposable. Even after the term indentured servant was no longer in use, this practice continued in the form of contract labor, thousands of Irish lives were lost building the nation's railroads and canals. There, life was so cheap that laborers who died were often buried in unmarked graves near the work sites, with no ceremony or recording of their deaths.

Smithsonian Magazine reported in its April 2010 issue that a mass grave containing the remains of 57 Irish immigrant workers was recently discovered in Pennsylvania. They probably died of cholera and were buried quickly with no ceremony, covered up so that the company wouldn't have trouble recruiting new workers. Similar burial sites lie alongside this country's canals, dams, bridges and railroads, their locations known and unknown; their occupants nameless, said the Smithsonian article. So common was death among the railroad workers that it was said that an Irishman was buried under every tie.

During the potato Famine in the mid-1850's, another huge wave of Irish immigrants came over, often agreeing to work as indentured servants or contract labor under whatever circumstances just to stay alive and not starve in Ireland. The Famine had been preceded by huge —clearances in Ireland. Between 1847 and 1854, over a quarter-million people were evicted from their homes. This was the result of the — Gregory Clause, which stated that no tenant who was inhabiting more than a quarter of an acre of land was eligible for public assistance, so the Irish, who could not subsist without assistance when the potato crops began to fail because Catholics also could not hold jobs other than agriculture, where forced to turn their land over to landlords. The landlords would then evict them, often with extreme force, and burn the houses and outbuildings to the ground so that they could not come back. They then were forced to die of starvation or disease or go to the workhouses, where they were often transported, or to agree to go to America as indentured servants no matter what the circumstances of that indenture might be. In some cases, the landlords themselves would pay for the tenants to emigrate on the aptly named coffin ships, whether the tenants wanted to go or not.

The Irish immigrants who fled to America were hated by many. Lodging houses turned them away and bars and restaurants refused to serve them. If they finished their indenture, they met signs everywhere saying, "No Irish Need Apply." Because of this, indentured or free, they had to take the hardest most dangerous jobs and were treated more harshly than other servants.

In the mid 1800's a non-Irish servant wrote home to his family, 'My master is a great tyrant, he treats me as badly as if I was a common Irishman.' The writer further added, 'our post in America is one of shame and poverty.' So if this poor soul was being treated so badly and he considers that he is being treated as a common Irishman, one can see what sort of treatment was generally expected for the Irish servant.

Many Irish immigrants arrived in America in the 1800's just in time to become embroiled in the Civil War. The statistics for the Confederacy are not clear, although some sources cite 40,000 Irish soldiers in the Confederate forces, but more than 170,000 are said to have fought for the Union. Many of these immigrants had not yet had time to get settled and find work before they were drafted, and others had been treated harshly and found only —No Irish Need Apply signs when they attempted to find employment. Despite all of this, many fought bravely. The all-Irish 69th New York Regiment gained especial fame for their bravery at Bull Run, Antietam, Gettysburg and Fredricksburg in particular.

When the Erie Canal was being built in New York City in 1818, at least a quarter of the workers were Irish. Thousands of Irish men moved into Albany to do work related to the canal, and while it is not possible to know how many of these were indentured servants, it is a safe bet that many of them were, and those who were contract laborers were not much better off. These men lived in barracks and shanties and worked from sunup to sundown, with a two-hour break for dinner. Because of the nature of the work, the poverty of the living conditions, and the drinking, violence, and gambling that always accompanies these sorts of conditions, the canal workers were considered the lowest of the low and avoided as much as possible by everyone else.

Even many slave owners would not allow their slaves to work on the canals, because it was too dangerous. It became a saying, according to Ireland and the Americas: "culture, politics, and history: Vol 2, from which I have drawn these facts, that —to build a canal four things were needed: a pick, a shovel, a wheelbarrow, and an Irishman."

According to Kirby A. Miller in Emigrants and Exiles, in the mid-1800's in Providence, Rhode Island, an average of 9 people lived in two rooms. In New York, as many as 75 people lived in 12 rooms, paying $4 a month for rent. J.F. Watts, in The Irish American, reported that some Irish families in New York lived in hovels for which they paid $3 a month rent, overrun with rats which spread disease from the overflowing sewage in the outhouses This took a great toll on children, with 2/3 of the deaths in New York in 1875 being children under 5, most of whom were Irish.

In 1900, the U.S. Census noted that 18.2, or nearly one in five, of the children in the country between the ages of 10 and 15 were working. This practice was not stopped until the passage of the child labor laws.

In the 1870's until around 1910, many Irish and Scottish men came over to America as labor gangs. In exchange for passage, the laborers signed an agreement with a contractor, with negotiated wages for them and kept a cut. The men signed willingly, not being afraid of working hard and believing that the was their way out of poverty, but they did not know that they were signing up for a life of dangerous, miserable work at little pay, with employers who had no care for their safety and cared only for their own profit.

Because the conditions in the mines was so horrible in Pennsylvania, the Irish miners formed a secret union called the —'Molly Maguires' to combat the mine bosses who kept them and their families as slavers and treated them brutally and with careless disregard for disfigurement or death to workers. They simply fought back with the same methods the mine bosses used against them. This made the 1860's and 1870's a time of unprecedented violence in the Pennsylvania mines, but it brought attention to the terrible conditions of the miners, both child and adult, and those who depended upon them. Despite the regrettable nature of the actions taken by the Molly Maguires, they did lead directly to the rise of larger, stronger and more legal labor unions, which led to improvements in conditions ranging from limiting child labor, raising wages, and limiting work hours to improving safety conditions in the mines.

"Irishmen also made up the majority of the workers on the railroads. This work was so dangerous that death was a daily occurrence, and workers were hastily buried in shallow graves along the rail embankments, while the work continued relentlessly on."

Rebellion

"The Irish did just not meekly accept their fate, whether enslaved or indentured against their will, or tricked into signing papers that promised conditions that did not materialize, or contract work into food by false promises. They developed very poor reputations as servants, because they were very prone to run away or to stir up rebellion."

Freedom

"After the Civil War, the Irish began to take on new and somewhat better occupations, although they were still often dangerous and underpaid jobs. The Irish had a near monopoly on the newly created jobs of policeman and firefighter, for instance and are still represented more than any other ethnic group in those professions. As horse cars and streetcars became popular near the turn of the 20th century, the Irish not only laid the tracks for them but many of them became the first drivers and conductors. By 1900, the Irish made up about a third of all the plumbers, boilermakers and steamfitters in the United States. The risk became involved in the unions early and that led to much political involvement. Many also sought careers in the Catholic Church as nuns and priests. In all these ways, through hard work, perseverance, and politics, and the Church, the Irish advanced in America."

These are mainly notes taken from many other sources. I am just concerned with giving you an idea thar there are many books – "Irish Slavery""The While Slaves" "White Slavery in Colonial America" – easy to find on the internet. Writers like Dee Masterson. "Labor in America", Foster Dulles. "18th century White Slaves" Daniel Meaders. And many more.

AUSTRALIA

"According to the article, —Irish Diaspora, 'in Wikipedia, 50,000 Irish men and women were transported between 1791 and 1867. Today, 33 to 40% of Australians claim Irish heritage, double the percentage of Americans who are known to have Irish ancestry. Many of these convicts were women and children. Indeed, according to the National Archives of Australia, about a quarter of the early convicts were under the age of 18."

CANADA

"After the war of 1812, many Irish Catholics came to Ontario and worked in the same unsafe and despised positions they worked on in the States: 'the railroads, the canals, building roads, and cutting lumber. Rather than being indentured or enslaved however, they worked for free land, and many of them actually received the Canadian land by which they were entitled to. Many others were tenant farmers, particularly around Peterborough in the 1820's."

"In general, however, it must be noted that those Irish who survived the journey to Canada and did not die in quarantine were more likely to successfully assimilate and subject to less mistreatment and prejudice than they experienced in the U.S., unless they worked in the mines. Many of the adults were fishermen, loggers, and other rugged outdoor workmen who were only expected to work hard but not to conform to the rules of urban society. Their different ways, their religion, and their language were no burden to them in the frozen North. And the children were, in general, better provided for and trained so that when they reached adulthood, they could enter the general population and support themselves."

Bangor

Light of the World

Kathie Walters

Bangor - Light of the World
Copyright © 2008 Kathie Walters

Printed in the United States of America

Published by Good News Ministries
220 Sleepy Creek Rd.
Macon, GA 31210

Scriptures are taken from the
NEW KING JAMES VERSION

Copyright 1979; 1980; 1982
by Thomas Nelson Inc.
Used with permission.

Format by Lisa Walters Buck
amstaf.designs@gmail.com

Table of Contents

Introduction

This account is a brief history of the Bangor Monastery. Bangor Monastery had about 250 years of non stop prayer and praise. The High Choir was famous all over the world. How did it start? Why did it stop? What happened in between?

Patrick Prophesies About Bangor

Patrick and his companions came upon a valley in County Down, Ireland. It is said that they "beheld a valley flooded with a heavenly light, and with a multitude of the host of heaven they heard, as it chanted forth from the voices of angels, the psalmody of the celestial choir." Patrick called it the "Vallis Angelorum" "Valley of Angels." In this place, at a later time, a famous monastery was built, whose "High Choir" celebrated continual praise to God, the like of which the world has never seen or heard. The praises were sung and chanted without ceasing for 200-300 years. There is a fragment of this precious ancient liturgy remaining in the Ambrosian library of Milan in Italy. Bangor Monastery was founded by a dedicated and powerful Abbot, Comgall, in 555 AD. Patrick prophesied of Comgall's birth and the foundation of the abbey at Bangor 60 years before Comgall's birth. Another Bishop, Macniseus of Conner, also prophesied the night before Comgall's birth, "He will be adorned with all virtues, and the world will be illuminated by the luster of his miracles. Not only will many thousands follow him, but many princes." (you can read more about Comgall's ministry in Bangor in Kathie's book "Celtic Flames" available at kathiewaltersministry.com)

The prophesies of both Patrick and Macniseus came to pass in detail. Bangor was respected throughout Europe as a great center of learning and a place of great light. The power of God was demonstrated in mighty ways through the ministry and boldness of Comgall. Signs and wonders were a part of his ministry even while he was a student under the famous Abbot Fintan. There were around 3500 monks at Bangor who preached with great signs and wonders following. The monasteries were like our present day Bible Schools. They did not consist of people locked away in seclusion, but rather they evangelized the United Kingdom and Europe.

The Dead Raised

One time one of the monks from Bangor went to visit a monastery in another part of the country, and while he was there, he died. Comgall ordered his body to be brought back to Bangor. When it arrived, Comgall prayed for him and he was restored to life. The monk told the other brothers what had happened after his departure from this life. "I was brought towards heaven by two angels sent by God, and while on our way, other angels came to meet us saying, "Bear this soul back to his body, for Comgall, God's servant, has requested it. Therefore bear it back to Comgall, with whom the monk will live to an old age."

Another time, a company of brethren, led by Columba of Iona, came by boat to visit Comgall. During the crossing, one of the monks died. When they arrived at the mouth of the river, Inver Beg, they were greeted and escorted to the monastery. Comgall washed their feet and asked if anyone was left on the boat. Columba said that there was one remaining, but that he would not be able to come unless Comgall himself went to fetch him. Comgall went at once to the boat to fetch the monk. When he arrived he found the dead monk. He was astonished, but he took to prayer at once. "In the Name of Jesus Christ arise, and hasten with me to your brethren." The brother monk arose and accompanied Comgall to the monastery. Then Comgall noticed that he had lost his sight in one eye. He declared that no monk should labor under such a defect and he bathed the man's eye. His sight was restored and he could see extremely well all the days of his life.

The dead were raised, the sick healed, and gospel preached with power across all of Ireland and Europe. There were so many monks desirous of being a part of Bangor that 3,500 students were taught at Bangor and its surrounding community.

Truly Comgall was a wonderful example of Christian piety, dedication, servanthood, and power. He demonstrated the Gospel with great authority and won the respect of the Kings and rulers. Critan An old man, an Anchorite named Critan, once visited Comgall during the Easter Festival. During the Easter service Critan saw a bright vision of angels. They touched the hands and mouth and the head of Comgall and joined in his benediction. Critan was very thirsty from fasting, and wanted in his heart to drink from the same cup as Comgall. Although nothing was said, the prophetic gift in Comgall was stirred and he knew the desire of Critan. After the service, Comgall entered his cell and took some wine. He then called a servant named Segenus and sent him with the wine to Critan saying, "Bear this wine to the holy man, Critan, who is now very thirsty, and let him drink from my cup, with thanks to God. Tell him from me, 'You are a patient and faithful man.'"

The Dead, Young Boy Raised

One day after a journey, Comgall returned to his monastery and found that a young boy had died during his absence. He said, "It is my fault that this boy has died before his allotted time." Approaching the body, he prayed and the boy was instantly restored to life. He asked the boy, "Do you desire, my son, to remain in this life?" The boy declared that he would rather go to be with the Lord in heaven, and Comgall imparted a blessing, and the boy peacefully yielded his spirit back to God.

A prince who was a great sinner came to the gates of the monastery with an offering of silver, but Comgall sent it back to him with a message saying, "Why do you wish to discharge your iniquities upon us? Bear your own crimes and fruits." Part of the fulfillment of Patrick's prophecy was the famous "High Choirs" which sang at Bangor Mor. Their strength came from the form of worship which they inherited originally from the early temple worship and later via the Desert Fathers.

The Desert Fathers

The Irish Celtic Christian Fathers, including Comgall, were very insistent that their spiritual inheritance was from "The true vine which came out of Egypt." Their revelation and monastic system was inherited from the Desert Fathers in Egypt, Anthony being the most famous of the desert monastics. The Desert Fathers saw their ministry as "gatekeepers of the nations." They lived and fought a spiritual warfare in the realm of the spirit that today we know very little about.

The High Choir

According to the scriptures, some kind of devotional worship was maintained both day and night for we read that singers, as well as the Levites, had their lodging in the temple house because they were employed in their work "both day and night." There is also a reference to the Perennial Praise of the temple in Isaiah 30:29, "Your song will then sound in the night when the feast is celebrated. And at the change of watch, "Bless the Lord, all ye servants of the Lord, who stand by night in the house of the Lord."

The Perennial Praise

The Perennial Praise was observed strictly by the Essenes (Community of the Righteous) from 200BC-200AD. The Rule, "Let among the many, keep awake in community a third, all the nights of the year in order to read aloud from the Book and to expound judgment and to sing blessings altogether."

And so during the night, as two thirds of their number slept in their tents the other one third kept up their continual chants of hymns and psalms. As the Laus Perennis constituted the old dispensation, so the Bangor Antiphonary constituted the new.

One of the reluctant soldiers of Constantine was a Hungarian named Martin. Martin became converted and eventually became the Apostle for Gaul. He was familiar with the monastic ideals of Anthony. He established a monastery or "White House" in Marmoutiers, and it was through him that the Laus Perennis was established in Briton. Among those who visited the monastery and took part in the Laus Perennis was a young man named Patrick!

Winning The Kings and Rulers

The monasteries established in Ireland in the 4th-6th centuries were powerful forces with which to be reckoned. Like our modern day Bible colleges, they trained and taught thousands of converts who went over the whole world preaching and praying and winning cities and towns to God. Their philosophy of winning the kings and princes to the Lord worked, as many leaders were won to the cause of Christ and consequently the people followed.

Patrick Raises the King's Two Children from the Dead

Patrick, for example, won Dublin to the Lord by raising the King's two children from the dead. Brigid, Cuthbert, Brendan, Keiran, Columba, Patrick, Comgall and many others trained thousands of young men and women, who went far and wide preaching the gospel and demonstrating the power of God to the heathen and the Druids. Open confrontations with the Druids were not uncommon.

It is said that the "High Choir" of Bangor was a light over Ireland. Day and night they sang psalms and praises and Antiphon Aries, continually watching and praising the God of their salvation. They released the power of God upon the land.

Berncard of Clairvaux Wrote of Bangor Light of the World in the 12th Century

"A place it was, truly sacred, the nursery of saints who brought forth fruit most abundantly to the glory of God, insomuch that one of the sons of that holy congregation, Molua by name, is alone reputed to have been the founder of over a hundred monasteries: which I mention for this reason, that the reader may, from this single instance, form a conception of the number to which the community amounted. So widely had its branches extended through Ireland and Scotland that those times appear to have been especially foreshadowed in the verses of David: 'You visited the earth and watered it; Thou greatly enriched it: the river of God is full of water: You watered the ridges thereof abundantly; You make it soft with showers: You blessed the springing of it.'"

Distant Lands

"Nor was it only into the countries previously mentioned but even into distant lands that crowds of saints from Bangor, like an inundation, poured forth. One of whom Columbanus, penetrating into the regions of France, built the monastery of Luxeuil, and there it became a great multitude. So great do they say it was that the holy continual praise was kept up by companies, who relieved each other in succession so that not for one moment day or night, was there an intermission of their devotions."

Columbanus

Columbanus was born in Leinster in 543, and he was educated in the islands of Lough Erne. Columbanus was highly educated, a scholar, later becoming an Apostle to Switzerland, France, and Northern Italy. He was given the greatest missionary commission and was sent from Bangor to Europe with 12 companions and from references from Columbanus' own letters, the names of most of them were recorded. Gall, who became almost as famous as Columbanus; Domgal, who acted as Columbanus' minister; and Cummian, Eunocus, Columbanus (the younger), Equonanus, High, and Libranus. Probably Anglo-Saxons Deicola, Caldwald, and Leobard were also included. The Bangor monastery was very international and after spending a little time in Britain, they eventually arrived at Burgundy, in Gaul in 590.

Authority of the Elements and Natural Realm

The early Celtic Christians exercised a great authority over the elements and the animals. It is told of Columbanus that one day as he walked and meditated in the woods, he was suddenly surrounded by several wolves, but he stood motionless and quoted "Deus in adjutorium." The wolves touched his garments and turned away.

Crowds came to hear the Irish preacher and the great foundations of Luxeuil and Fontaines were laid under his great ministry. For 20 years many hundreds of the children of the nobles of the Franks and Burundians were taught and discipled by him.

Columbanus Opposes the Queen of Burgundy

Columbanus opposed the Queen Regent of Burgundy, Brunehault. She presented Columbanus with the four sons of King Thierry (her grandson). They were sons of his concubines, and she asked Columbanus to bless them. He refused! Brunehault from that moment declared that she would see to it that Columbanus came to an end.

At the same time, Columbanus stood his ground with regard to the Celtic tonsure and the Celtic celebration of Easter. Both were very sacred to the Celtic Fathers. The Gallic bishops followed the customs of Rome in both respects and strove to reduce the fearless Irishman to conform to their own practices. Columbanus not only refused, but sent a long epistle to the bishops in synod. "I am not the author of this difference; I have come into these parts, a poor stranger, for the cause of Christ, the Savior. I ask of your holiness but a single grace: that you will permit me to live in silence in these forests, near the bones of the 17 brethren I have seen die. Oh, let us live with you in this land where we are now, since we are destined to live with each other in heaven. I dare not go to you for fear of entering into some contention with you; but I confess to you the secrets of my conscience, and how I believe above all, in the tradition of my country, which is besides that of Jerome."

Columbanus Arrested

Columbanus soon had to pay the penalty of his bravery. His monastery was regularly boycotted. The inhabitants were forbidden to have any dealings with him. He was arrested and confined to Besancon, from where he soon escaped to Luxiel.

An officer and detachment of soldiers were sent to arrest him. They found him in church, chanting the service. "Man of God, we pray you to obey the King's orders, and to return from whence you came."

"No," answered Columbanus, "I cannot think that having left my country for the service of Jesus Christ, that my creator wished me to return." He was arrested and had to leave his beloved Luxeuil. He was hurried across France and put on a ship bound for Ireland.

But though man proposes God disposes and the ship was flung back upon the sands of the mouth of the Loire. The captain believed that somehow Columbanus was an unlucky passenger and landed him at the nearest shore.

Columbanus' quarrel with Brunehault and Thierry kept him out of the greater part of France, and so he set his heart to bring the Gospel to Northern Italy, which was already filled with the Arian heresy (the Arians were disciples of Arius, a theologian who came to prominence in 318. He taught that Jesus, being a son, was not eternal and did not exist before his natural birth. His theology was refuted by the church at the council of Nicea in 325).

Columbanus took refuge with Clotaire II, son of Fredegund, but his heart was really set on Italy. He finally went by way of the Rhine River and landed at the mouth of the Lake Constance. He stayed and preached and taught and established the monasteries of Reichenau and St. Gall, which to this day is one of the richest repositories of Irish MSS and Irish literature in Europe.

St. Gall

St. Gall was a companion of Columbanus. In preaching the gospel to the Swiss, Columbanus often broke the boilers in which they prepared beer and offered a sacrifice to Woden. At times, he burned their temples and broke their images. Of course, such behavior provoked opposition. Columbanus was driven from place to place and was refused food by local inhabitants. But such sturdy missionaries were not daunted by such behavior. They continued to erect their huts and plant their gardens.

Waters Spirits

Columbanus made nets and Gall, the learned and eloquent preacher, flung them into the lake to no avail. Then Gall heard a demon from the mountains calling to the demons from the lake. "Here I am," answered the water demon. "Arise then," answered the other one, "and help me chase away these strangers who have expelled me from my temple; it will require us both to drive them away." "What good should we do?" answered the demon of the lake. "Here is one of them upon the waterside whose nets I have tried to break, but have never succeeded." He prays continually and never sleeps."

Gall spoke to them and said, "In the Name of Jesus Christ, I command you to leave these regions without injuring anyone."'

Then Gall came ashore went to the church; but before the first psalm had been sung, they heard the yells of the demons echoing around the tops of the surrounding hills, at first with fury, and then losing themselves in the distance.

Success attended the ministry of Columbanus in Switzerland and even greater success attended his disciples. But he was not satisfied and felt he had not yet attained that to which his soul had been prepared. Finally the people tired of the preaching and complained to the Duke that the Christians scared away the game of the forest with their prayers and presence. They stole his cows and killed his monks.

Crossing the Alps

Columbanus and another monk crossed the Alps over the St. Gothard pass and arrived at the court of Agilulf, King of the Lombards. There he was received with great respect and endowed with the church and territory of Bobbio, in a gorge of the Apennines, between Genoa and Milan. An old church dedicated to St. Peter was in existence then. Columbanus restored it and added to it a monastery. He established the perennial praise in his monasteries which had come down through the tradition of the desert fathers and from Bangor.

Despite his age, he shared the labor with the others, and under the weight of his bent old shoulders, he carried the enormous beams of firwood. This Abbey of Bobbio was his last ministry. He made it the citadel of orthodoxy against the Arians, lighting there a great lamp of knowledge and instruction which long illuminated Northern Italy. The monastery existed there over 1,000 years until it was suppressed by the French in 1803.

Columbanus Dies

Columbanus and his monks evangelized the Arians and pagans all around. At the end of his life, Columbanus returned to the solitude he loved. He found a cavern on the opposite shore of Trebbia which he transformed into a chapel. Like other Irish Anchorites, he spent his last days alone, waiting on his Lord, until "God called" his fearless servant home on November 2, 615.

On Columbanus' deathbed in the Valley of the Appenines (near Bobbio) he sent his staff back to St. Gall who had left Ireland with him in the beginning of his journey to Europe. He died on the 23rd November, in the year of our Lord 615 AD, around age seventy-three. His remains are enclosed in a stone coffin and are still preserved at the old monastic church at the old monastic church at Bobbio. He was consumed with a great zeal for God, the source of his immense power.

Belfast

The great monastery on the shores of Belfast Lough lay open to attack by the Vikings. They first raided the shores in 810, and between the years of 822 and 824 the tomb of Comgall was broken into. Its costly ornaments were seized and his bones were taken from their grave. St Bernard said that in one day over 900 monks were killed.

It is unlikely that the Laus Perennis were ever sung again at Bangor. The order of Columbas did not long survive its founder. It merged with the Benedictine order in the 8th century. In honor of St. Gall, there arose a monastery which became one of the most important centers of Irish learning on the Continent.

Finally, in the biography of Malachy, St. Bernard wrote of his friend (Malachy) that he attempted to revive the church at Bangor. The church was again attacked by Conor O'Laughlin, King of the Northern Ui Neill and the city was destroyed. Malachy was forced to migrate south and founded a work in County Kerry.

In 1134, he was called back to Ulster to become Archbishop of Armagh and in 1137 he returned to his beloved Bangor. He later died in the arms of St. Bernard on All Saints Day, 1148. Bernard wrote, "Malachy, as if he had been taken up out of our hands by angels, happily fell asleep in the Lord in the 54th year of his life in the place and at the time he had chosen and prophesied."

Bishop Reeves wrote that in the end Bangor fell very far short and...'that the emphasis was on the High Choir instead of Evangelism,' and it finally dwindled and became but a name and a shell of what it once was.

The Bangor Antiphonary and other Irish books were moved to Milan. Today there is preserved in Milan a reminder of the days of glory when the Laus Perennis was sung in Ireland and Bangor was the great LIGHT OF THE WORLD. For many centuries ago, in the days of the Anglo -Normans, there existed in Ireland a tradition which was already an ancient one.

Revival Comes Through Preaching the Gospel with Signs and Wonders

It is written in history that Bangor became known all over the world for the High Choirs and psalms and songs that were written. But the Perennial Praise and choirs were a by product of this great move of God that touched France, Switzerland, Italy, Spain, Germany, etc The revival came through amazing signs and wonders which accompanied the preaching of the Gospel.

When the attention gets on the by-product, marvelous though it be, the anointing is replaced gradually by another atmosphere. The atmosphere has power-singing and music can produce an atmosphere of comfort and excitement, similar to the anointing. The enemy is subtle, crafty. Be watchful-keep your eyes on Jesus-and on His command to us to preach the Gospel. It's easy to replace the preaching of the Gospel with other things that are, or appear to be, spiritual. We are to disciple, to teach, to bring those outside to a knowledge of Him--the Lord of Glory.

We are to worship. Of course we are. We should love to worship and praise, but it is not instead of doing as he told us, "Preach the Gospel, heal the sick, cast out devils, and establish the kingdom."

Learning from History

There is so much we can learn from history: How revivals came, what happened? How God's presence comes among us in resurrection power? But we also must learn from the mistakes our predecessors have made so that we can avoid them. God's desire is to dwell among us, not just to visit us. Visitations are wonderful and marvelous, but His desire is that we live in His glory and go from glory to glory.

"I will walk in them and dwell in them, and I will be their God and they shall be my people, says the Lord," 2 Cor 6:16.

Songs of Psalms

The monks of Bangor and other monasteries seemed to have songs and poems for every occasion imaginable. Contained in the remnant of the Bangor Antiphonary are several beautiful songs and poems. Part of the Voyage of Bran speaks of the birth of Christ:

A great birth will come after ages, That will not be in a lofty place, The Son of a Virgin Mother, He will seize the rule of the many thousands. A rule without beginning, without end, He has created the world, so that it is perfect, Whose are earth and sea, Woe to him that be under His unwill It is He that made the heavens, Happy he that has a white heart, He will purify hosts under pure water, It is He that will cure your sickness.

"The Commemoration of our Abbotts" is probably the most valuable, because the date of the manuscript can be determined by it. It is very interesting that as you can see, after the introductary verse, the lines run in alphabetical order.

You can see a fragment of the Bangor Antiphonary that is preserved in the Ambrosian Library of Milan, Italy.

See also Celtic Flames and Columba- <u>The Celtic Dove</u> from my website www.kathiewaltersministry.com

References

<u>Bangor Abbey Through Fourteen Centuries</u> - The Rev. James Hamilton, M.A

<u>Ireland and the Celtic Church</u> - Professor G.T.Stokes D.D.

<u>Lives of the Irish Saints</u> - Reverend John O'Hanlon

<u>Bangor Light of the World</u> - Ian Adamson

<u>Celtic Flames</u> - Kathie Walters

Child Prophets of the Huguenots

Excerpts and accounts of the prophetic move
of the Spirit in France 1688-1702 from the
French book
"The Sacred Theatre of the Cevennes"

Commissioned by Kathie Walters
by Francois Maximileon Mission
Translated by Claire Uyttebrouck

Child Prophets of the Huguenots
Copyright © 2016 by Kathie Walters
Originally published in 1707 by Robert Roger

Additional authors include:
Elie Marion, Durand Fage, and Jean Cavalier

ISBN:1-888081-33-3
978-1-888081-33-6

Printed in the United States of America

Published by

Good News Fellowship Ministries
220 Sleepy Creek Rd
Macon, GA 31210

Format by Lisa Walters Buck
amstaf.designs@gmail.com

Table of Contents

Introduction

First published in London in 1707, this book is a collection of testimonies about the "Small Prophets of the Cévennes," these young boys and girls, sometimes infants, who called the Protestant people to repentance and later on to resistance.

This book highlights a little known prophetic movement which took place between 1688 and 1702 in the South of France (Drôme, Vivarais, Cévennes and Bas Languedoc).

These witnesses, who were also fighters, affirm their unwavering convictions and tell how they became prophetic, and how their prophetic gift led them to take arms to fight for their freedom of conscience. Many of them went into exile in England, Switzerland, Holland and Germany.

Children Caught Up in the Spirit

Suddenly, at the end of the 17th century, in the area of the Cévennes, babies stood up in their cribs and called people to repent. Young children of three and five, teenagers of twelve, fifteen, and seventeen rolled around on the floor and prophesied, announcing the deliverance of the people of Israel (meaning the Protestants (Huguenots) and the destruction of Babylon.

When caught up in the Spirit, the children spoke the language of their Bible, French, although their mother tongue is the local Patois. They could neither read nor write. Children and adults alike didn't remember what they said when they came back or they only remembered very little. Everything started in the Dauphiné with a shepherdess, in 1688. Isabeau Vincent, fifteen years old, spoke with her eyes closed, commented on the Bible and called sinners to repent. People listened to her. She was arrested, thrown in jail, but she kept preaching.

In 1689, a young peasant boy called Gabriel Astier prophesied and drew crowds to himself. Then hundreds of children, sometimes only three or four years old, "fell in a state of ecstasy". Nine month old babies prophesied in their crib. Some children prophets were denounced by their parents to the authorities, arrested and thrown in jail. Some of them escaped, then were adopted by the Camisard families.

Louis XIV revoked the Edict of Nantes in 1685, and after that, the Protestant faith was forbidden. Pastors were deported out of France. Massive forced conversions to Catholicism began. Persecutions were fierce and deadly, but the prophetic movement spread. In the beginning it was entirely peaceful, the "small prophets" (small because of their young age and size) called the people to reconcile, to repent, and to a completely break off from the Catholic Church. Then, in a second stage, prophecy became warlike.

Mazel, a simple peasant from the Cévennes, was the first one to call people to "holy war" and to avenge against the torturing clergy. They had the right to have people hanged, beaten to death or imprisoned for life. It was the Holy Spirit who told Mazel to take arms, and it's by His revelation that the Camisards heard about traitors among them, avoided ambushes, discover conspiracies, and hit their enemies. All their decisions were inspired by the Spirit. Thanks to this, a group of simple peasants regularly defeated a trained army.

Prophetic Troops

The leaders among them were the most prophetic men, and at least half of the troops had the gift of prophecy. They didn't need watchmen, for it was the Spirit who warned them when there was danger. Some fighters had the gift of prayer and exhortation, others received warnings for the Church, and still others received specific warnings for specific situations. The more they listened and obeyed, the more victorious they were. All of them had an incredible zeal for God's glory and totally yielded to His will, whether in life or in death.

Pastors

At the time, the Catholic authorities ignored the pastors. They thought they where the same as priests. They thought that if the Pastor is no longer there to take care of the flock, the sheep will waste away and scatter.

One only had to observe what a pastor truly was in any given village to see the difference with a priest. The big difference was that Protestants read their Bible every day. The pastor's role was quite clear: he's the most instructed brother and helped the others to better understand the difficult passages of Scriptures. He was the guide who acknowledged the full autonomy of his brothers' faith and helped them grow into their full potential. Instead of being God's spokesperson like a priest, he was the wise man -- the expert of the community who encouraged the others.

Prophets said that when they were taken up in the Spirit, it was something wonderful and divine. They started shivering and feeling weak -- as if feverish. They would yawn several times and then fall down and close their eyes. They stayed down for a while then they suddenly woke up and started prophesying. They said they saw the open Heaven, angels, paradise, and hell. Prophets prophesied not only during assemblies, but also in the countryside or in their houses. Small assemblies gathered, 400 to 500 people, major ones 3,000 to 4,000. For several years, they gathered in the woods, in caves, and in other isolated places. They all preached repentance, this is a theme found in all testimonies. The Bible was quoted in French by people who cannot read or write French, and who hardly knew French.

When Isabeau, the fifteen year old girl, was in prison, she prophesied more than ever. She told her torturers that they may kill her, because God will raise up many child prophets who will tell even greater things than she does.

Responsible for Self &
Child Prophets

Each person, by reading the Bible, becomes his own priest. The Gospel can be spread without clergy, without religious authorities, without hierarchy. Pastors having been deported, the lay people filled in by simply devoting more time than others to the needs of the church.

Every person is responsible for himself and co-responsible for the community, irrespective of institutions, which is a deeply democratic and indirectly revolutionary concept.

Because "churches" had collapsed due to persecutions, there were no more pastors and no more fundamental freedoms. So little groups popped up and tried to make up for this institutional void.

In an assembly, a witness saw a young girl who could hardly read. She said she couldn't preach, but the Spirit preached through her. She started praying and her prayer was so beautiful he thought he was seeing an angel. Then she sang a Psalm and she sounded like an angel. She then started preaching and what she said was so beautiful, so zealous, and so full of wisdom that it was obvious it was divine. She quoted the Old Testament and the New Testament as if she knew the whole Bible by heart. She illustrated passages with such accuracy that everyone was dumbfounded. She lamented on the state of the church and said, "It's due to our sins." Then she comforted the people in an incredibly gentle way and promised mercy, peace, blessings, fulfillment, and eternal joy to all those who received the Lord.

Another witness mentions a girl from Languedoc, who received revelations. When she was in the Spirit, she was capable of saying things about this witness that she could not have known naturally. An angel "stirs her organs and gets her to say what the Spirit orders."

Jean Vernet testified in 1707 that the first people he saw in the Spirit were his mother, his brother, two of his sisters, and a cousin. His mother, ignorant of only the French language, spoke it when she was in the Spirit. While visiting friends, he saw a fourteen month old baby prophesying in French, although this child had never said a word before. The baby spoke with a loud voice and called people to repentance. There were about twenty people in the room and everyone was cut to the heart and wept. He also heard about an infant, not yet weaned, who prophesied in the same way. It often happened that these small prophets warned the assembly that they needed to break up because soldiers were coming. When they didn't heed that word immediately, they were caught, thrown in prison or sent to the galleys.

Thousands of children prophesied and the Catholic authorities claimed they were impostors and they were taught what they were saying. These children were tortured, flogged, the soles of their feet where burned, but they kept prophesying. They were brought to a Medical School to be examined, and from time to time they were seized by the Spirit and began to prophesy. It is obvious that those children were totally illiterate and that their discourse didn't match their age or their level of instruction, as they could quote the Bible and say things they obviously had never learned. They ended up being called fanatics.

A Man Named Mazel

As prophets filled the jails, the court gave the order to stop imprisoning, and to simply slaughter those who still gathered together. Only then did the people start to take arms to defend themselves, and only after a man named Mazel received the order from the Holy Spirit to do so.

Thousands of women didn't stop prophesying and singing hymns, although they were being hanged by the hundreds. Several witnesses mentioned slaughtered brothers who "had the honor to suffer martyrdom." Everytime those who were being mistreated, imprisoned, and tortured -- seem full of joy, sang hymns, and prayed to God continually.

Two witnesses told two different stories, where people in the Spirit said that God would destroy Babylon (the Catholic church) and restore His Church. These people couldn't read and yet they spoke French well when in the Spirit.

One witness said he went to a place where he was told an assembly would be taking place, but when he got there with a few friends, the place was empty. When they prayed to find the meetings and a bright light appeared in the sky, like a big star, and led them to where the assembly was, about half a mile away. Another witness said that it was the light in the sky that enabled him to find his way back to his regiment of Camisards.

Among the troop of Camisards, Mazel fell into a state of ecstasy and announced the imminent death of one of the brothers during combat. Once he "woke up," he identifies the brother about to die and advised him to get ready. This brother accepted the news with resignation, and a few weeks later he was mortally wounded by a bullet.

In fact, all the brothers in the troop who were called to die, either during combat or because they would be executed, were warned in advance by the Spirit, so that they could say their goodbyes to their family and prepare to glorify God in their death as they had during their lifetime. The Spirit was by their side until their last breath, which for them, was simply a passage from one life to the next.

But most of the time, the Camisards received words of knowledge telling them they have nothing to fear in combat, and they would all come back with incredible stories of bullets being caught between their shirt and their skin without having wounded them. As a result, bullets were as inconsequential as rain to them, and young boys of twelve fought the "lions" with their sling, just like David with Goliath. They all lived in the most serious purity and discipline, and as the Spirit forbade them to take any spoil, they sometimes burned true treasures.

In a home, a witness saw a six year old boy fall in the Spirit and prophesy that a part of the great Babylon would be destroyed. Another boy of eight prophesied that the Protestant faith would be re-established in France. In the assemblies, some people spoke what sounded like a foreign language, and then someone else "interpreted."

A witness said that a young girl of eighteen prophesied to him that he would be arrested the next day, but he that didn't have to fear because he would be released that same day. That's exactly what happened.

Sometimes, those in the Spirit saw armies of angels. At times these angels fought against armies of demons in the sky. It was prophesied on several occasions that God would have fires or lights fall from the sky during the night to blind the eyes of the enemies or to guide His people, and that's what happened.

A young girl fell in the Spirit and prophesied that there would be many ordeals in the land, but a "new world" would arise. She interceded so that the country will not be struck by lightning, and started to weep tears of blood. Some people who knew her well said that it was not the first time they saw her shed tears of blood.

"Beginning on August 24, 1572 and lasting for nearly two months afterward, tens of thousands of men,
women and children were slaughtered across
France...in a religious war."

source: http://www.todayifoundout.com/index.php/2014/03/
st-bartholomews-day-massacre/

Account of Jean Cavalier, Head of the Camisards

Jean said that he joined an assembly gathering in a barn out of sheer curiosity, for the things of God didn't interest him. When he got there, a little boy was shaking in the Spirit on the floor and he inwardly laughed at him. The little boy then said that there were people in the assembly who only came out of curiosity, with a mocking spirit, and he portrayed Jean so accurately that he was ashamed and headed towards the door to leave. At that moment a second young boy fell in the Spirit, right in front of the door, making it impossible for Jean to leave. The boy talked about a malicious person trying to leave. Jean was all the more uncomfortable, until he heard another child preach in such a way that it cut him to the heart and he started to pray. All fear left Jean and he asked God to get to know His will. God's zeal fell on him. The child preached with such conviction that the whole assembly was in tears. He preached for about two hours and nobody missed a minute of it. Everyone knew that the child could not read, didn't know any French (although he taught in French), and didn't have the education to say what he said.

Jean was deeply converted by this child's words and wept profusely when he was confronted with his sins. Then he felt like a hammer hit his chest and fire spread through his veins and into his whole body. He lost balance and fell down. The heat intensified, the fire increased, and he shook uncontrollably. He remembered his sexual immorality and was convicted of sin like never before. Meanwhile, the child kept preaching and said that he was blessed to have been called by God to be filled up with His grace, and that he needed to thank Him with a grateful heart. As he grumbled, the child went on to say that God's will was to hold him for a while before receiving spiritual gifts, and in the meantime he needed to pray unceasingly.

Jean went back home totally transformed, still in tears and sometimes losing balance as if he was drunk. He stayed in that state for nine months. God's hand often touched him but his tongue is still tied. However, God's grace comforted him as he obeyed the Spirit who prompted him to pray. Sin no longer tempted him, nor was he drawn to Catholicism.

After nine months of tears and shaking without words, Jean fell into an exceptional state of ecstasy and God opened his mouth. For three days he was in the Spirit and didn't eat, drink, or sleep. He only preached and urged people to repent, and all the people who saw him were convinced that it was the Spirit speaking through him.

He then decided to join the Camisards, peasant fighters, prompted by the Holy Spirit to fight the King's army which slaughtered Protestant men, women and children without mercy. One day he was sitting down at table with his comrades in arms and received a word of knowledge that there was a Judas among them who intended to poison everyone. Another brother received a word that the traitor intended to poison the water of the cistern. A third person received the revelation that the traitor still has the poison on him and would try to hide it or throw it away, but he will be unmasked and exposed...

...And indeed, the traitor was confronted by someone who learned from the Spirit exactly where the poison was hidden, and went to get it. But they decided to let him live and release him. The traitor then denounced everyone to the authorities and Jean is made prisoner with about 60 of his comrades.

Painting of Jean Cavalier

source: https://commons.wikimedia.org/wiki/File:Jean_
Cavalier_chef_camisard.jpg

Jean is Made Prisoner

Jean travelled on a ship and found himself in the midst of a great storm. One of the prisoners received a word saying that within four hours they would arrive safely, and that's what happened.

In the jail where they were imprisoned, they saw the traitor again. He had a dream where he falls into a heap of garbage and choked to death. A few days later he became ill and literally vomited garbage and died.

Some time later, Jean was released from prison although he had been sentenced to life in prison. He went back home. During the Sunday worship, the head of the assembly, brother Clary, was seized by the Spirit and learned that there were two traitors in the group who only came to spy, but they would be unmasked. Indeed, the Spirit led him to the two traitors, who immediately repented and said it was out of poverty that they were working for the enemy. Clary has them bound, but the Spirit told him people were grumbling because they believe that if the traitors repented so quickly, it is because Clary was their accomplice.

The Holy Spirit then addresses the assembly through Clary and convicted them of their lack of faith. The Spirit says that in order to show them His power, He's going to put Clary on a stake to be burned but he would not be affected. The assembly pleaded to not burn him because they didn't believe that he was going to survive.

A stake was built and Clary positioned himself in the middle. Someone lit it and the flames were higher than his head. When the flames died down, Clary got out unharmed, without even the smell of smoke in his hair or clothes. Then the traitors were released.

Painting of a group of Huguenots in hiding:

source: https://en.wikipedia.org/wiki/Karl_Girardet

Calling Everyone to Repentance

Another witness told the story of a young girl, ten to twelve years old, who fell in the Spirit in the house of a gardener. When she started talking, she told everyone to keep quiet because in the garden there was a man who could betray them. The gardener went out and saw a surgeon, a known persecutor, collecting plants for a remedy. Once the surgeon was gone, the girl started to preach, calling everyone to repentance, which would bring a shower of blessings on all. However, if they kept sinning, the country will be hit by the most terrifying judgments from God. This girl spoke in French, although she had never studied it, and quoted many passages from Scriptures, although she couldn't read.

A few months later, the same witness saw people rushing to a house as he was walking down the street. He followed them and saw a girl who had just fallen in the Spirit. She said approximately the same thing as the former girl and finished up with a long and beautiful prayer.

A few days later, he went to visit a young girl, six or seven years old, accompanied by a priest. She was seized by the Spirit and started to preach. The priest couldn't believe his ears. When she "woke up," he tried to convince her to tell him who taught her those things, but she claimed she doesn't control anything she does or says, it wasn't her but something that "takes over". The priest realized that it was ridiculous to see any malice in this child, or in any child preaching or prophesying that way, but because of his position, he feels compelled to say it was by the power of the devil that those children spoke the way they do.

Another witness said that it was "the village half-wit" who preached best and had the most beautiful sermons. She could not speak four words of French and was normally very shy in public. The witness said: "This Balaam's donkey has a mouth filled with gold when the Spirit speaks through her." No speaker was listened to the way she was, and no audience was more captivated or moved. Her eloquence flow was a pure wonder. This woman could control when she fell in the Spirit. When people came to visit her and hear her preach, she just needed to say a short prayer and the Spirit came to "take over", and the Holy Spirit preached and prophesied through her.

Another witness told the story of a young girl of eight or nine who regularly fell in the Spirit. At those times, she only breathed through sighs, her breast was heaving and all her body was shaking.

Other Christian Historical Books by David & Kathie Walters

Columba - The Celtic Dove

This book is about St. Columba of Iona, an island of the coast of Scotland. Columba had a monastery there where he taught and trained hundreds of young men to preach the Gospel, heal the sick, raise the dead. This book is filled with eyewitness accounts of Columba's amazing prophetic gift, the miracles, and many angelic visitations. It was first compiled by St. Adamnan around 692-A.D. – 697 A.D..

Celtic Flames

This book is about the amazing lives of seven great saints:

Brendan of Clonfert 448 A.D.-581 A.D.

Cuthbert of Landisfarne 634 A.D.– 687 A.D.

Columba of Iona. 521 A.D.- 597 A.D.

Brigid First Abbess of Kildare 453 A.D. – 524 A.D.

Patrick The Celtic Lion 389 A.D.-471 A.D.

Comgall Abbot of Bangor 516 A.D.-601 A.D.

Kieran, First Bishop of Saiger 352-A.D.-540 A.D.

Bangor Light Of The World

Much of our present day 24 hour IHOP have been patterned on this history of Bangor. This account is a brief history of the Bangor Monastery. The monastery had around 250 years of non stop prayer and praise. The High Choir was famous all over the world. Many people were sent out from there to take the Gospel into Europe How did it start? Why did it stop? What happened in between?

Children Aflame With The Spirit

Amazing little known accounts from the journals of John Wesley. 1703-1791 A.D. Wesleyan Revivals with children from 1730-1780, including modern day Revivals with children for more than 40 years in the ministry of David Walters.

What Happened To Evan Roberts And The 1904 Welsh Revival?

Like a tree shaken by a mighty storm, Wales was moved by the power of God until almost every home in the nation felt its impact! So great was the fear of God, conviction gripped the people and in some communities crime disappeared. God used a young 26 year old Bible student, Evan Roberts. Read what happened and how this most amazing move of God which covered Wales began to wane and change. Why did the revival go? What happened to Evan Roberts? Why did he start having nervous breakdowns? We need to know these things and not make the same mistakes in the future.

Bright And Shining Revival

An account of the Hebrides Revival 1948-1952. The Hebrides Islands are a small group of islands off the west coast of Scotland. In 1948-1952 God poured out His Spirit in response to a handful of praying men and women. It doesn't take multitudes to move the hand of God but those who are determined to push through the crowd and touch the hem of his garment. Whole towns were saved as the presence of God chased people Kathie Walters visited the islands and the people several times to obtain first hand knowledge of the revival.

The Irish Slaves In America

Most people in America are ignorant of the huge indignity and cruel treatment of the Irish Catholics. Why is it so hidden? Why isn't it taught in schools as many Americans are from these very immigrant people who were forced to come to the U.S. as slaves and many died in the process? Over 800,000 men, women and children, were sold as slaves.

Teaching CD's by Kathie Walters

Getting Free and Living in the Supernatural

In Depth for Seers and Prophets

Spiritual Strategies

The Almond Tree

The Fanatic in the Attic

Faith and Angels

Revival Accounts and Getting your Family Saved

Other Books by Kathie Walters

Living in the Supernatural

The Spirit of False Judgment

The Visitation

Parenting By the spirit

Angels Watching Over You

The Bright and Shining Revival

Seer List

Elitism & The False Shepherding Spirit

Health Related Mindsets

Contact:

Kathie ministers in churches, conferences, and women's conferences. She believes that the realm of the Spirit, the supernatural realm, the angels, miracles etc. are meant to be a normal part of the life of every Christian. The religious spirit prevents Gods people from receiving their inheritance.

For further information on Kathie or David Walters ministry visit:

Website: http://www.KathieWaltersMinistry.com

E-mail: kathiewalters@mindspring.com

or write or call:

Good News Ministries

(478) 757-8071

220 Sleepy Creek Rd.

Macon GA 31210

Tour of Ireland & Scotland with Kathie Walters

Come to Ireland and Scotland on a 14-Day Celtic Heritage Tour with Kathie Walters!

- Re-dig the spiritual wells of this beautiful country
- Pray on the Hill of Slane where St. Patrick lit his Pascal fire and defied the High King.
- See the place where St. Patrick first landed to bring the Gospel to Ireland by God through the Angel of Ireland, Victor.
- See the green hills and dales of Ireland - a picture you will never forget.
- Visit the ancient places of worship that will help enable you to grasp hold of your godly inheritance.

Then on to Scotland

- Tour the beautiful highlands of Scotland.
- Visit the island of Iona, where St. Columba built his monastery. See beautiful Loch Ness and Loch Lomond and visit Edinburgh.

Made in the USA
Columbia, SC
27 May 2022